John Terrell Fry

photographs by
Nancy Nolan

STEWART, TABORI & CHANG
New York

candlelit christmas

**Decorating with Candles
for the Holiday Season**

Project Editors: Sandra Gilbert and Trudi Bartow
Designer: Alexandra Maldonado
Production: Kim Tyner and Alexis Mentor

Published in 2003 by
Stewart, Tabori & Chang
A Company of La Martinière Groupe
115 West 18th Street
New York, NY 10011

Export Sales to all countries except Canada, France,
and French-speaking Switzerland:
Thames and Hudson Ltd.
181A High Holborn
London WC1V 7QX
England

Canadian Distribution:
Canadian Manda Group
One Atlantic Avenue, Suite 105
Toronto, Ontario M6K 3E7
Canada

Library of Congress Cataloging-in-Publication Data
Fry, John Terrell.
Candlelit Christmas / John Terrell Fry; photographs by Nancy Nolan.
    p. cm.
ISBN 1-58479-294-9
1. Candles in interior decoration. 2. Christmas decorations. I. Title.

NK2115.5.C35F789 2003
747'.93—dc21

2003044915

The text of this book was composed in Akzidenz Grotesk.

Printed in Singapore.

10 9 8 7 6 5 4 3 2 1

First Printing

A portion of the proceeds of this book will be dedicated to Potluck, Inc., Arkansas' only food rescue organization. Potluck feeds more than 70,000 children and adults each year.

contents

preface

The anticipation of Christmas is perhaps one of our earliest memories: the tree is decorated, the wreath is hung, the gifts are wrapped, and the first guests will soon arrive. As the candles are lit, the entire house glows with a quality of light that sets the tone for the most wonderful time of the year.

When we decorate we can recapture that childlike faith of fantasy and dreams. Inviting us to dream are candles surrounded by holly and dancing ribbon. Shiny bright ornaments, nestled among a hundred tiny lights, are as mesmerizing as a Victorian gazing ball.

Just after the Thanksgiving turkey is carved, I begin planning my Christmas decorating. The following weekend I select my tree from the neighborhood nursery and begin taking inventory of lights, ornaments, and of course, candles. Some of my favorite decorations I use year after year, while others are reinvented with new design applications. This year I found a stash of handmade bead and jewel ornaments that I have not used for several years. These intricate decorations will set the theme for my tree.

Growing up on a farm, we always cut our own tree and collected natural materials for trimming the house. I have not strayed far from this practice. My favorite aspect of decorating is collecting Mother Nature's endless supply of berries, branches, nuts, cones, and greenery.

Attic-stored ornaments matched with a favorite garden urn and fresh greenery let me enjoy a mix of seasonal favorites. Candles provide the unity and warmth to enhance these unusual partners.

A candle on the windowsill extends the lights from the Christmas tree and insures a marvelous welcome. All through the house, elegant candelabras or simple votives capture the season with light and flickers of movement. Our senses are heightened, as the mundane becomes magical. We feel that wonderful childhood innocence returning.

Throughout this book, I suggest including your guests and children in your holiday decorating efforts. With a little imagination and planning, the experience will make everyone's holiday more memorable—and echoes of these trimming memories will enrich all the holidays to come.

I hope this book inspires you to dream, imagine, and enjoy your own candlelit home this Christmas and many more.

John Terrell Fry

christmas with nancy

It would be the first Christmas for Nancy in her new house. New to her but in reality a turn-of-the-past-century historic house that she shares with her husband, photographer Steven, two sons, Park and Henry, and their dog, Elvis.

A classic bay window in the dining room provides the perfect setting for the Christmas tree. Embellishing the massive windows with a garland of fresh mixed greenery outlined the space. We decided to let the white woodwork and the greenery set the color theme. A trip to the country provided another key element: tallow berry branches that appear to have pearls on each tip.

When working with a two-color theme I enjoy using different hues, so we selected ornaments and trims from silver-green to lime. The effect, as you can see, is dazzling.

For the table and mantel we remained faithful to our color story. Vintage sixties florist vases of milk glass found at a tag sale became the home for votives and flowers. Classic urn shapes elevate luminaries and the candlelight takes the edge off the stark white pressed glass. Clipped boxwood and towering tallow flank the mantel. For the table, snowballs of white hydrangea are put on pedestals and guarded by their own deep green foliage.

We marked each plate with a place card secured to a hostess-gift ornament and lit the way with a goblet containing a candle. We also tucked a nosegay of tallow and boxwood under the napkin ribbons.

As the daylight is replaced by candlelight the tree and the entire setting become golden and appear to be of the same era as the house. The moment is magic.

A silver ice bucket bubbling over with ornaments reflect the candlelight. OPPOSITE Polka-dot ribbon keeps the spirit light and repeats the shape of the berries and baubles. Santa's gingerbread snacks stand out for easy spotting in the dark.

The snowballs of
hydrangea perfectly echo
the milky-white florist
goblets. Together they
provide the ideal centerpiece
for a cozy dinner.
RIGHT Inspire your guests
to build their own holiday
decorative collections
with these elegant hostess
gifts of Christmas
ornaments.

Reflections of candlelight dance through the ivory ribbon of the tallow wreath on a timeworn kitchen chair. OPPOSITE By candlelight the crisp white and cool green ornaments turn golden as the evening progresses.

Pull together candles, ornaments, and
trims to create a coordinated color theme
for holiday decorations. OPPOSITE Tag
sale '60s florist vases of milk glass reflected
in the mirror over the mantle provide a
classic touch to luminaries.

terry's christmas tree at 1205 kavanaugh boulevard

Holiday greetings at my home begin at the garden gate. The antique ironwork creates the perfect background for a fresh cedar wreath. Outdoor candle lanterns flank each side. White fairy lights and hanging glass votive holders enhance the rose arbor, which has been draped in cedar roping.

A garden chair dressed with assorted greenery holds a hurricane lamp filled with red candles. I accented my eggplant-painted front door with a simple wreath tied with a shimmering purple ribbon.

Entering my attic with the courage of Indiana Jones I spot the stacks of boxes of decorations and ornaments that have not been seen for a year or more. Opening each one I delight in memories of past Christmases. I discover a box in the back that I do not recognize. Closer inspection reveals handmade ornaments of faux jewels and beads. A Fabergé-inspired egg of cottage origins inspires me. Colors will be jewel tones and silhouettes will tell the story.

Mimicking the ornaments I use candle spheres of tufted gold and ruby glass salt dishes for tea light holders. A trip to the farmer's market provides the natural jewels of cranberries, pomegranates, and kumquats. These will echo the ornaments, playing the roles of garnets, rubies, and topazes. No glue is needed here. Foam forms and toothpicks allow everyone to take part in the creations of topiaries, which will serve as focal points in front of the tree.

I choose a noble fir tree and use a garden urn filled with wet sand to insure freshness. Red mercury-glass finals reinforce the importance of classic silhouettes and allow the jewels of the Nile to sparkle.

Charming hand-made ornaments purchased from a church fundraiser bring an array of color and sparkle to store bought treasures. OPPOSITE As suggested by its name, the noble fir stands proud with limbs reaching straight out. This allows plenty of space for ornaments to hang and turn at will.

TOP This cranberry topiary was created by a holiday guest. Present all the materials on a cloth-covered table and let your guests decorate. BOTTOM Ruby red and gold votive holders create the light that pulls the decorations together.

The crown jewels of cranberries, pomegranates, kumquats, and leathery magnolia leaves stand as a grouping on the cocktail table.

A garden urn filled with moist sand allows the tree to stay fresh and stand tall. It also allows plenty of room for presents. I gathered nandina branches and sprayed their foliage with gold floral paint. Using wire I secured the bunches close to the trunk to provide a background for the decorations.

nancy's red, white, and green party

The weather outside is just what we wished for! The drifts of snow cover the porch and all its holiday greenery. We add red candles and take the indoor colors outside. Gardenia foliage borrowed from the ancient shrubs outside the guest quarters cools the sharp silver and vibrant reds. A crisp setting of holiday spirit is evident. The often-misunderstood red carnation gives life to red tapers and red gazing balls. These ornaments, presented atop silver goblets, hold in miniature all of the magic of Christmas.

A paper plate becomes a charger when gardenia leaves are glued around it and a simple white plate is placed on top. Of course, your holiday dinnerware would work just as nicely. This grounds the simple tree of gardenia tips that are inserted into a foam cone. The texture of a white matelassé table cover is the perfect snowy ground for the table. It is time to get out the silver and let the candles show off your recent polish.

Simply pairing a shimmering ornament with a silver goblet can create holiday gazing balls. OPPOSITE The beauty of lush gardenia leaves makes even everyday dishes special.

inspired by nature

My garden is ready for winter and now it is time to light it for holiday entertaining. With mesh Christmas lights I cover the boxwood hedges and then add glass hanging votive holders to the tree branches. Floating candles are placed in the fountain. Everything is done in advance. If we are lucky enough to have snow it will be even more wonderful.

The outdoor chores complete, I decide to do a little extra pruning in the garden. An armful of boughs later I tackle the table in my front entry. A hand-carved angel found on a trip to San Miguel, Mexico, was placed in the entry to greet guests. Wings spread and a branch of laurel held high, she casts a gentle mood for all. Silver-point drawings from Russian artist Victor Koubak and a vine, cone, and nut wreath grace the wall and offer more good tidings. Delicate ivory candles with nature reliefs flicker. The refrectory table is laden with native magnolia, elaeagnus, ivy, and fir. This suggests a woodland setting that allows the real-life bird's nest a befitting forest. The fragrance of the natural greens and soft vanilla candles greets everyone.

ABOVE I found a bird's nest in one of the trees and placed it on garden greens. A pine cone-shaped candle and almonds for eggs give light and interesting texture. RIGHT Floating candles combine the elements of fire and water. As the temperature drops it will become fire and ice. OPPOSITE The slick trunks and branches of the crepe myrtle trees provide the perfect holders for votive cups. The snow came and made the night bright and the candles look like stars.

Throughout this tablescape weath-
ered iron plays out harmoneously with
the natural foliages and neutral candles.
The sculptural form of an artichoke makes
an exquisite candleholder which beautifully
integrates the candles and the greenery.

The hand-forged iron and glass votive holder glows with the feeling of an ancient cathedral window. As the flame recedes behind the amber glass it provides a soft glowing effect. OPPOSITE A poured candle surrounded by hazelnuts and incased in an oversized hurricane brings nature and light to eye level. The cut-glass pattern refracts the flame and gives the illusion of multiple candles.

adrienne's berry merry christmas

Decorating in Adrienne and Brad's home we chose natural materials to reflect their love of nature and to echo their careers as landscape designers. Bountiful fruits and berries of pyracantha were used to enhance their collection of artifacts, which give the house warmth and character. A carefully edited collection of pumpkins left over from the fall holidays gets all dressed up for Christmas with fresh berries and wired ribbon crowns. The glow from John Bell's time-worn candlesticks, made from pealing architectural fragments and prisms from chandeliers, brings everything together. Wire topiary forms in the shape of pineapples were filled with oranges, given a collar of magnolia leaves, and topped with mottled candles the color of the oranges. The pair flanked the mantel. At their feet we used nandina berries and apples cored to hold tea lights.

For the centerpiece I selected a lion's head planter in burnished gold and used only the pyracantha berries. I chose iron floor candlesticks to flank one side of the fireplace and repeated the lush berry branches as embellishments. The candles used here are ivory. This color theme honors the crisp, white lines of the mantel and creates several levels of candlelight.

Adrienne has two opposing primitive cocktail tables. On one I placed a wreath of fir and berries around a handmade pottery candlestick. The other table was topped with an antique sleigh landscaped with fresh and dried materials. A few white berries give the hint that we wish for snow.

In the library a mission-style chair in front of a rich, walnut armoire becomes a whimsical setting for the season's offerings. The chair seat becomes a stage for walnuts and apples with tea lights glimmering and berries underneath the antique bread tin container. Wood, nuts, berries, and fruit are beautiful and artful. Simple elements so unexpected.

Candles placed at different levels create
a balance of light and transform the room and
decorations into a cozy holiday respite.

44

An antique wooden sleigh provides the perfect setting for greenery, fruits, and berries. The graceful trinity of pillar candles pulls nature's bounty together as the focal point of the table's decorations.

These apple tea lights evoke the wholesomeness of a country Christmas and remind us of the bounty of the season.

terry's christmas dinner

We all love to transform our dining room and create a special atmosphere for our guests. A festive table tells my guests how happy I am to have them in my home.

When the room glows with candles and transformed lamps, everything works together. The silver candlestick lamps become part of the season's decoration when the shades become topiaries. I removed the silk shades that are normally on the lamps. Then I purchased shade frames and wired magnolia and nectarines to them. With a flick of a switch the lamps become trees glowing over the table. To balance the light, candles are used at their base and scattered down the dining table. A boxwood garland winds the length of the surface. Vietri Rosso Vecchio handcrafted terra-cotta dinnerware is matched up with pomegranates, cranberries, apples, and nectarines. The red swirls on stemware catch the candlelight and shimmer. The nickel foot tub holds a bounty of fruits and nosegays of red roses. Fresh cedar garlands are the evening's drapes. With the twinkle of the candles and the sparkle of conversation the setting becomes magical.

Wire frames for lamp-
shades are covered with
magnolia leaves and
nectarines. A garland of boxwood runs the entire length
of the table. By keeping the
center decorations low you
can ensure intimate dinner
conversations.

renee's soirée

Collections of holiday decorations are cumbersome to store but well worth the effort. Renee's ever-expanding collection of tree toppers provide the dining room with spires worthy of angel-guarded castles. Get out all of those old brass candlesticks you meant to sell in your next yard sale and with hot glue you can secure the toppers in place. After the season is over, simply run hot water over the contact point and the glue will let go.

An Indian sari gathered in the center of the table creates golden clouds and sparkles with its own stars. Candles in amber Moroccan hurricanes bring the light and color to eye level. Beaded glass baskets hung from the chandelier dance with the light overhead. This gives the room balance and romance. Each napkin wears a beaded necklace and supports a golden tassel. Sharing the plate with the napkin is a hostess gift: a julep cup of terra-cotta and tangerine roses monogrammed and dated for each guest.

We decided to dress up the mantel in the living room. Fortunately we still have more toppers. In the center, Renee's vintage angel floats above the shimmering treasures. On each end, temple jars hold fountains of elaeagnus and magnolia. Fresh greens provide a lawn and gold tapers light the way. In the fireplace is a simple collection of candlesticks with white tapers.

The rich colors of the library just off the living room support the pair of wood carved angels. Above is an oversize vine wreath with bunches of mercury-glass grapes. Square red pillar candles of different heights were stenciled with gold motifs. Red cathedral glasses glow from the candles within and make this a place for reflection.

Dressed for the holidays, these candles keep
their ornaments in the glow of the season.
Odd trims, ribbon fragments, and costume
jewelry makes these pillar candles take
center stage even though they are placed
in the background.

The golden wings of the splendid angel seem
to move as the candles reflect and play across
them with the music of light.

A julep cup of terra-cotta and tangerine roses becomes a hostess gift. OPPOSITE A stenciled pillar candle appears to repeat the motif of the china pattern. A small wreath of glass berries completes the setting.

john and the pepper-mint twist and red hot polka dots

Ellen's five-year-old son John has a sweet tooth. When you are creating candleholders and vases out of candy canes the ones that break are fair game. While gluing the candy to an ordinary drinking glass there were a few casualties.

We placed votives in the small containers and a handful of red carnations in the larger and tied the vases with a red satin ribbon. We made snowballs of white carnations and snowflake mums. We surrounded white candles with a collar of snow made of flowers. John decided since the flowers have no stripes, we should use Red Hots as polka dots. The next evening we let John pick out the order of wooden alphabet blocks that we glued onto a straw wreath and foam cone. Tiny brown teddy bears and shimmering ribbon united the primary colors of the blocks. The scale was perfect for him and we also had a lesson in the letters. Together we created keepsake decorations and memories to last a lifetime.

The warmth of candles allows us to simultaneously look to the future with hope and remember the past with fondness. Our quality of life is greatly enhanced by family customs and traditions. We spend this special holiday time together and the candles and decorations lift our spirits and lead us to the beauty of the season.

This snow globe doesn't
have to be shaken—the candle
creates the movement.

Looking good enough to eat, these light-hearted mini carnation and snowflake mum snowballs will bring a smile to faces young and old.

projects

Silver Candlesticks with Tallow Berry Nosegays

Although any ribbon will do for this project, a polka-dot pattern will complement the berries nicely. Silver candlesticks offer a spirited contrast to the glowing flame.

TO MAKE

step 1   Tie berries into bunches with string, being sure to leave enough length to tie in ribbon and secure to candlestick holders.

step 2   Tie ribbon to each nosegay; wrap remaining ribbon around candlestick holders into a bow.

step 3   Stick candles in decorated candlesticks.

YOU WILL NEED

Tallow berry sprigs

Waxed floral string

6 to 8 candlestick holders

Assorted ribbons

6- to 8-inch taper candles

note: If tallow berries are not available, bitter sweet is a great alternative.

Topiary with Oranges and a Candle

This festive decoration creates a one-of-a-kind centerpiece that is not only beautiful but edible as well.

TO MAKE

step 1 Fill topiary with fresh navel oranges.

step 2 Insert the candle at the top.

step 3 Wire magnolia leaf tips in place at neck of the topiary to create a collar.

step 4 Lay nandina berries at base of the topiary.

YOU WILL NEED

20-inch wire topiary, shaped like a pineapple

2 dozen navel oranges

3- by 6-inch pillar candle

Wire

Wire cutter

3 magnolia leaf tips

Nandina berries

Tree Toppers

This is the perfect way to display any extra tree-topping ornaments you may have. It is quick and easy, and you don't have to worry about ruining your favorite piece. Disassembly is a snap.

TO MAKE

step 1   Apply small amount of hot glue to bottom of tree topper.

step 2   Place the ornament on top of a candlestick holder and hold in place 30 seconds so glue can set.

step 3   When you are ready to disassemble, hold the candlestick holder under hot running water until the glue loosens.

Garden Urn with Artichoke Candleholder

A candle rests inside as the heart of this artichoke, proudly displayed in an antique garden urn. This ensemble gives a new twist to the typical floral arrangement.

TO MAKE

step 1　Gently pry apart artichoke leaves with your fingers. Remove the choke with a sharp knife, being careful not to pierce the leaves.

step 2　Fill the garden urn with the floral foam.

step 3　Cut the artichoke stem at a sharp angle and insert it securely into the foam.

step 4　Place the glass votive cup with a candle inside the artichoke.

step 5　Wind ivy around the base of the artichoke to cover any exposed foam.

YOU WILL NEED

One large artichoke

Sharp knife

5 1/2-inch iron (or ceramic) garden urn

Floral foam

Glass votive cup

1 votive candle

12- to 15-inches ivy vine

74

Topiaries of Fruits and Berries

These bright and cheery topiaries combine fresh and
festive elements of the season.

TO MAKE

step 1   Secure the round foam topiary to the footed container with
          florist clay.

step 2   Starting at the bottom of each foam core, insert toothpicks
          spaced to size of the fruit.

step 3   Pierce the fruit onto the toothpicks.

step 4   Continue piercing the fruit until each foam core is completely
          covered.

step 5   Add leaves to the top and bottom of the topiaries for desired
          effect, inserting the stems into the foam core.

75

Snowball of Mini-Carnations

These snowball decorations won't have you worrying about water drips on the coffee table. Adding the Red Hots will lend just the right amount of whimsy.

TO MAKE

step 1   Place the foam cube on a plate or saucer.

step 2   With a knife, cut a circular hole large enough for the glass holder to rest in.

step 3   Place votive holder in the foam cube.

step 4   Cut the carnations, keeping 1½-inch stems.

step 5   Insert the flowers into the foam until the foam is completely covered.

step 6   Sprinkle the Red Hots on top of the carnations.

YOU WILL NEED

Floral foam

Dessert plate or coffee saucer

Sharp knife

Glass votive holder

1 bunch white mini-carnations

3-inch cube of wet floral foam

1 package Red Hot candy

Crown

This decorative crown is fit for a king or a queen. Through candlelight, the cranberries take on the look of bright rubies.

TO MAKE

step 1   With florist clay, secure dry foam sphere to container or cakestand.

step 2   Cut hole large enough to hold the glass votive holder in the foam top.

step 3   Place each magnolia leaf vertically on sphere with tip of leaf at base of votive holder. Secure each leaf with 3 toothpicks, one each at top, middle, and bottom of leaf.

step 4   Place cranberries on the end of each toothpick.

step 5   Overlay and repeat until sphere is covered.

step 6   Add cranberries to the ends of toothpicks to cover any exposed foam.

YOU WILL NEED
Florist clay
5-inch dry foam sphere
Footed container or cakestand
Glass votive holder
8 to 10 magnolia leaves
Wooden toothpicks
Bowlful of fresh cranberries

Candy Cane Vase

Here's a peppermint twist on ways to liven up floral bouquets.

TO MAKE

step 1   With the glue gun, gently glue a candy cane to the exterior wall of the drinking glass, pressing gently for 10 seconds to set in place.

step 2   Continue this process until the glass is completely covered with candy canes.

step 3   Tie the bright red ribbon around the glass and secure with a dot of glue.

Apple Votive

Red delicious apples are perfectly paired with candlelit votives.

YOU WILL NEED

Tea lights

Red apples

Pen

Paring knife

TO MAKE

step 1   Hold the tea light on the top of the apple (apple must be able to stand up by itself). With a pen, trace the circumference of the votive onto the apple.

step 2   Using a paring knife cut out the circle. Core a hole large enough to accommodate the light.

step 3   Place the tea light inside the hole.

Lampshade Topiary

Wire lampshade frames are covered with magnolia leaves and nectarines.

TO MAKE

step 1   Cut magnolia branches to height of shade.

step 2   Wrap shade frame with magnolia branches. Secure with wire.

step 3   Insert florist picks into fruit and wire the fruit to frame.

step 4   Repeat step 3 until frame is fully covered.

YOU WILL NEED

Wire lampshade form

Magnolia branches

Florist paddle wire

Wire cutter

Wired wooden florist picks

6 nectarines or red apples

Ribbon Candle Holders

These decorative touches make any plain glass candle holder into a special gift of holiday magic.

TO MAKE

step 1   Cut ribbon in lengths to go around glasses, leaving an extra 1/8 inch to turn under at seam.

step 2   Glue the ribbon to the glasses.

step 3   Place tea lights or votive candles in each glass.

YOU WILL NEED

Assorted ribbon and trim

Small drinking glasses

Glue gun

Tea lights or votive candles

Alphabet-Block Tree and Wreath

This Christmas tree is perfect for a child's room, or any room. The child in all of us will appreciate it.

TO MAKE

step 1   Glue one side of each block to the cone in concentric circles, going upward. Stagger each ring to achieve a checkerboard look until the cone is completely covered. Follow similar pattern for the wreath.

step 2   Glue the mini balls between blocks.

step 3   Add the bears to top of tree and the wreath.

step 4   Tie a ribbon in a bow and glue to the blocks and the bottom of the wreath.

YOU WILL NEED

Glue gun

Three packages of children's
wooden alphabet-blocks
(for tree and wreath)

14-inch foam cone

10-inch straw wreath

Small red rubber balls

Mini teddy bears

Red ribbon

Gardenia Tree

This simple and elegant mini-Christmas tree will enhance any dining room tabletop.

TO MAKE

step 1   Secure cone to pedestal bowl with florist clay.

step 2   Wire leaves to wooden picks.

step 3   Work from top to bottom, and then side to side, until cone is completely covered.

step 4   Tie ribbon in a bow and secure with wired wooden pick.

YOU WILL NEED

10-inch foam cone

Pedestal bowl

Florist clay

Wired wooden florist picks

28 to 36 gardenia leaves

Ribbon

note: For a special touch, fruit and flowers can be added.

candle care

Here are a few simple steps that will ensure that your candles burn brighter, cleaner, and longer. Most of today's candles come with burning instructions. It is important to follow these guidelines.

wicks

- To avoid black smoke: Trim the wicks down to ¼ inch before burning.

- To prevent off center wicks: When you have extinguished a candle insert a spoon handle beside the wick and press until the wick is centered.

wax removal

- Wood or glass surfaces: Heat hardened wax with a hairdryer for a few seconds or until soft and then scrap away wax using a credit card.

- Carpet: Place newspaper over hardened wax. Using an iron on the lowest setting, gently press until the newspaper absorbs all the wax. Repeat if necessary.

- Fabrics: Remove as much of the wax as possible with fingernails. Then stretch the fabric over a colander and secure with a rubber band. Using a teakettle, bring water to a boil and pour over the wax area until it liquefies.

- Glass candle holders: Place in the freezer overnight and tap upside down until wax pops out.

storage

- A closet or drawer is an ideal place because of the dark, cool atmosphere.

- Tapers should be placed flat and wrapped in paper to protect from bowing and scrapping.

- Avoid direct sunlight as it will fade the wax color.

- Do not refrigerate candles as it may cause them to crack and burn poorly.

TIP: If your candle becomes nicked or scrapped, simply polish with a nylon stocking until the finish is even.

IMPORTANT TIPS FOR BURNING CANDLES RESPONSIBLY

A few simple measures will ensure your safety while you enjoy your candlelit home. Burn your candles mindfully. Always place candles in or on proper nonflammable candle holders, well away from any flammable material. Direct drafts can cause uneven burning. Keep lit candles out of the reach of children and pets. Trim the wick to 1/4 inch before lighting or relighting. Remove any foreign objects, such as matches and wick trimmings, from the wax pool. Allow candles to cool before relighting. Never move a lit candle, as the melted wax may spill. To extinguish candles use a snuffer, or cup your hand an inch or two behind the flame and blow gently. To remove candles from decorative, reusable candle holders, place the holders in the freezer for a short time, which will cause the wax to contract and pop out.

Most important, always be sure to extinguish all candles before going to bed. NEVER leave burning candles unattended.

acknowledgments

HOMES, GARDENS, AND ACCESSORIES: John Bell, Anncha Briggs, Phil Cato, Todd Estes, Thom Hall, Carol Herzog, Keith James, Park Lanford, Stephen Lanford, Sam Murphy, Patrick Phillips, Brett Pitts and Kevin Walsh, Renee and Scott Rittlemeyer, Ellen and John Scruggs, Jon Stone, Ken Stone, Adrienne and Brad Taylor, and Rus Venable

BUSINESSES IN LITTLE ROCK, ARKANSAS: The Accessory, At Home in Arkansas, Bear-Hill Interiors, Cabbage Rose, Fifth Season, Hocott's Garden Center, Massimo, Nola Studios, Tipton & Hurst, and Wordsworth Books

OTHER BUSINESSES: Bougainvillea, Atlanta, Georgia; Jim Marvin Enterprises, Dixon, Tennessee; New Creative Enterprises, Milford, Ohio